PEOPLE
DISCOVERY

Christina Lattimer

Presents

The 6 Secrets of Great Emotional Intelligence
For Inspirational Leaders and Managers

The 6 Secrets of Great Emotional Intelligence

For Inspirational Leaders and Managers

By Christina Lattimer

Published by People Discovery

United Kingdom

www.peoplediscovery.co.uk

ISBN 978-1-4717-0456-7 – The 6 Secrets of Great Emotional Intelligence – For Inspirational Leaders and Managers (Paperback)

Copyright

If you discover any information on our pages which you believe to be inaccurate or inappropriate, please notify us by sending a message to info@peoplediscovery.co.uk

Any references and examples quoted have been carefully although not substantially changed to protect the identity of any individuals referred to.

Dedication

This book is dedicated to my three children, Donna, Melanie and Daniel. The secrets in this book are the key to unlocking your true self. That is all I wish for you.

May peace joy, love and happiness be with you in everything you experience.

Table of Contents

Introduction

One of the most important skills you can develop to be a great people leader or manager and make your journey of life easier to navigate is emotional intelligence. During my 30 year career, I have through experience, self-reflection and investigation learned 6 vital secrets to great emotional intelligence.

Inspirational Leaders and Managers have great emotional intelligence

These 6 secrets are based in great wisdom and have been known and practised by our most influential leaders throughout history. They are not the main reason that great leaders have been successful, but they have been a major and necessary factor.

The basis of some of the secrets may seem very different to how you have thought before, and you may have long formed beliefs that make you sceptical or reject the information you are about to read. But on a deep level, you know that there is at least some truth in what you are reading and why you need to know this information right now.

We aren't born with an instruction manual

Unfortunately as human beings we aren't born with an instruction manual about how to live successfully. We learn through a series of taking in information, interpreting the information and reacting and then seeing the results. In other words, we learn as we go.

You know the saying that "the benefit of hindsight is a wonderful thing". Well that's because once we have experienced the results of our interpretation and reaction, we quite often would do things differently!

And so it is with emotional intelligence. There is no easy quick fix because we often have to learn through trial and error.

> **We are all at different stages of learning and that is OK!**

You may already practice some of the secrets or the concepts may be totally new to you. Whatever your beliefs, I hope you take something valuable away with you. Learning the 6 secrets may help you immediately and bring instant revelation. For some of you it may take some time for the meaning and significance of the secrets to filter into your awareness and experience.

For some, you may simply not accept the ideas within the secrets. If this is the case, then please ask yourself what seems like an irrelevant question, but which actually has great significance. The question is: "Would you rather be right, or happy?" Too often we choose to maintain our beliefs and thinking patterns and therefore our emotional state because we prefer to "be right", even if the very beliefs and thoughts we are maintaining are making us downright unhappy.

Wherever you are in your understanding of emotional intelligence, remember it is where you are meant to be. There is no right or wrong way to be, there is only where you are right now, with a willingness to learn, and that is absolutely fine.

How this book can help you

The 6 secrets I reveal can help you in a number of ways. Firstly, they can aid and help develop your own emotional intelligence. If you are like me, you are committed to life-long learning which not only means increasing your knowledge and skill base, but also means personal growth.

You can use the secrets to help you lead and manage your teams. The secrets lead to a greater understanding and acceptance of how people tick. This is very valuable information and can help you in the many situations you find yourself involved, in relation to managing your team.

Finally, the secrets can help you build better relationships both at home and in the workplace. Practicing the secrets will help you form more positive relationships both by giving you some strategies for how you relate personally, but also understanding how others relate.

How to use this book

There is a logical sequence to the concepts in this book and one idea builds on another. It is best to read through the secrets and absorb the information as it is presented. However, if a particular secret grabs you, and your instinct is to start there, then go for it! There is no right or wrong way to learn from the information in this book.

So without further ado, here are "The 6 Secrets of Great Emotional Intelligence – for Inspirational Leaders and Managers".

PEOPLE
DISCOVERY

SECRET 1

Secret 1 - Emotions are a guidance system not a result

Our natural state is a positive one. We know we are aligned with our natural state when we feel emotions such as happiness, love, peace, forgiveness and gratitude. This is just an example of some of the positive emotions we experience when we are being our true selves. Every decision we make in life has the potential to help us to align with our natural state. Sometimes we achieve that alignment and sometimes we don't.

> *Our true self is naturally happy, peaceful and loving.*

We truly are designed to be happy. As humans we have an operating system which takes in information, interprets it and then we make decisions about what we think about or how we feel. Our emotions are our inner guidance system which tells us whether we are on the right track to being aligned with our true selves.

We are always experiencing emotions. Sometimes we are aware of them and sometimes not. When you wake up in the morning, you can have a range of moods, from feeling grouchy, or exhilaratingly happy or even worried. A lot of us identify with our feelings, so we may say I'm a happy person, or I'm an angry person. Or we identify others by their emotions. For example we might say: he's happy-go-lucky or conversely, she's a misery.

Emotions are not a fixed state, or a fact. Emotions are a moveable feast, giving us vital information about whether the thoughts and beliefs we have are aligned with our true self.

Identifying ourselves or others with emotions is a mistake.

Many people believe that emotions are a result of an event or in response to something happening in our lives. We often believe that emotions are triggered in us by something that someone else has done or said. But this is not true. The truth is; our emotions are a signal to us, letting us know that the interpretation we have put on the event is not in alignment with our true selves.

We've all heard of SAD haven't we? It is Seasonal Affective Disorder. Simply put, it's a dark mood which is attributed to the lack of sunshine in our lives. What greater proof that events are the trigger for our feelings and emotions? But as we will find out later, actually our feelings and emotions are giving us information, not our response to information. The mood which is in place when suffering from depression or SAD or stress for example *is valuable data.* It is like a compass, but we think it's a barometer.

A friend of the family was always unhappy; she had experienced a couple of broken relationships and was constantly bemoaning her lot to anyone who would listen. She was greatly respected and cared about so she had plenty of support. The problem was, the support consisted of commiserating with her about the bad behaviour of others in her relationships. She was blaming her emotions on her experiences. After all, if it weren't for the bad behaviour of her significant others, then she would be happy. The truth though, if she had been able to accept it, would truly have set her free from her unhappiness, because her state of unhappiness wasn't as a result of the behaviour of the men in her relationships; it was giving her valuable information about her reaction to the behaviour.

Our emotions are a guidance system letting us know whether we are aligned with our true selves or not

I remember working with a lady who was due to get married. She was planning the wedding and sharing her delight with everyone regularly. One day, the wedding day looming, or so I thought, I asked her if she was getting excited. She smiled shortly and quickly apologised. "I'm sorry, I haven't really announced anything, but the wedding isn't happening" I was floored, and immediately concerned. I wanted to make sure she was alright and was looking for signs of tearfulness or despair, but there were none.

She told me that her fiancé had been offered a job in a city some 300 miles away and he wanted to take it. She said that it did not feel right for her, and that she concluded it was not the life she wanted for herself. So they re-evaluated their plans, realised they wanted different things and called the wedding off. I asked her if she was upset, and she told me that although she would miss him, and she cared for him a great deal, it was a blessing they discovered their differences before they got married. She waved him off wishing him luck, and about a year later she married a lovely man, who wanted to live in her home town, which matched her vision for the future. You can see the contrast from the earlier situation.

We blame situations or people for how we feel, but our feelings are always our responsibility

It is the same in the workplace. We blame situations or people for making our working life unhappy or stressful. There are many dynamics which exist, maybe people are feeling overwhelmed, or micromanaged or simply bored and demotivated. If you notice, there are people who work for you or with you, who even in the most adverse of situations remain calm, motivated and effective. There are others who will be stressed, negative and unhappy. The information from the adverse situation is the same, but the emotional experiences are different. We think that it is just because people are different and that some people cope better than others. The truth is, that people actually interpret information differently, and it is the interpretation which makes people feel differently about what is in essence the same information.

Grief is a terrible state to be in, and when we lose someone we love, it is really almost the ultimate event which can appear to engender great unhappiness and sadness. There are however stark contrasts in responses to losing a loved one. Loss is always sad. It can sometimes feel devastating for people, so please don't think I am undermining anyone's experience. As one who has suffered much loss, I am only too aware of the raw emotions which can result.

I worked with two women who both lost their mothers in the space of 6 months of each other. The responses couldn't have been more different. The first lady was off for 5 months. She was depressed, had counselling and eventually came back to work, and even 5 months later regularly broke down in tears. The loss of her mother had been a hard blow. The second lady was back in the office after a week. When I enquired if she was alright, she looked a little teary and told me that she was devastated and she was worried about other family members, but she felt that she was better distracted at work and that she knew this time would pass.

Both of these ladies had valid reactions to their losses, and as a leader or manager you must respect that this is where they were both at. However, healing for any situation can occur, even losing someone close to you when you realise that it is not the event, it is the reaction to the event which is where we need to focus our efforts. Grief is natural. Prolonged and debilitating grief is always because the focus is on the event, and not the reaction to the event.

Focusing on healing the emotion rather than the event which seemed to cause the emotion is the response in alignment with our true nature

In both of the separate scenario's above, if the people involved who had the most debilitating emotional response had focussed on their emotion as a guide, rather than a result, then they would have been motivated to examine their thinking and beliefs which caused the prolonged grief, and healing and the beginnings of improving emotional intelligence could begin much earlier and deliberately.

It's important to realise that the road to emotional intelligence can be a long one, and that often people feel out of control and do not realise that they can help themselves in a more proactive way, especially when they suffer great loss. Additionally, we must respect their own journey and not try to force healing onto someone. The secrets are intended to give you a new way, so that you can, if you wish use some of the techniques to grow emotionally.

Unfortunately, most of are scared of our emotions, we label them good and bad, healthy or unhealthy. We are sometimes afraid to look at "negative" emotions, and so we distract ourselves or repress them, or we become overwhelmed by them and hope they will just go away. The truth is, and what great leaders know, is that emotions are neither negative or positive, they are simply giving us feedback about whether our thinking is on the right track or not. Which leads us to the next secret; your feelings are a response to your interpretation of information.

PEOPLE
DISCOVERY

SECRET 2

Secret 2 – Your feelings are a response to your interpretation of information and interpretations can be changed

As discussed earlier, when we are feeling sad, or angry or even happy or joyful, we usually link this feeling to an event. I remember having my first baby. What an occasion, I felt joyful, full of love and caring for this beautiful little being. I was on cloud nine for months. I truly felt I was lucky and blessed.

Around the same time, a neighbour and friend of mine gave birth also. Unfortunately she was absolutely overwhelmed by the sheer responsibility and change that this little life was going to make, and she became depressed and withdrawn. Finally she was diagnosed with postnatal depression and was given some much needed help. This is another example of two similar experiences with a very different emotional reaction.

> *The same experience can engender different emotions depending on our interpretation of the experience*

It's really important to stress at this point that there is no right or wrong emotional reaction. It is simply our inner guidance telling us where we are. For a leader or manager, your task is not to force someone to develop emotional intelligence, judge them for experiencing a negative emotion, or judge a reaction or belief. It is for you to understand the process that your people are going through; accepting everyone is different, and giving the right kind of support.

My 14 year old son was recently involved in a car accident. He was hurt, but not seriously. He was running for the school bus and did not see the car. The car was pretty badly damaged and the driver shook up. I was really concerned for the driver. I was at pains to point out to the police that it wasn't his fault. My son was cut and badly bruised, and he had a couple of trips to the hospital, but miraculously had no serious injuries.

Soon afterwards I got a letter from the driver's wife threatening me with court action unless I paid for the damage to the car. My first reaction was anger, and a real sense of injustice. I was fuming that in a situation where I had been keen to avoid casting the finger of blame on the driver that he turned the tables and was seeking to secure damages from me. The first 10 minutes I got lost in my negative emotions. Then I realised what I was doing, I was focusing on the event. I had been magnanimous in my desire to make sure the driver was alright, and this was how I was being repaid!

You can choose to interpret events and situations in your life however you like

I took a deep breath and realised that I was reacting to my interpretation of the event, not the actual event itself. I immediately calmed down and began to think rationally about the situation. I realised that the driver's action was nothing to do with me. He was entitled to do what he thought fit and I needed to have faith that all would turn out well. I was immediately able to change my initial thinking and therefore my emotions about the event changed too.

Like it or not, many people make decisions based on how they feel about something. Sometimes this can have disastrous consequences if there is faulty thinking behind the feeling. Revenge and some crimes are committed because of the way people feel.

Psychologically, we are in two camps. Carl Jung's work "psychological types, was made famous by the work done by Myers and Briggs, the mother and daughter team who developed the Myers Briggs Type Indicator tool. In Jung's work, he identifies two diametrically opposed ways we make decisions. We either make decisions because of how we feel about something, or we make decisions about what we think about something.

We also use both decision making preferences at different times and in different situations. No-one always makes decisions through feeling, or indeed thinking. We simply have a preference to use one way which is more comfortable to us.

I am predominately a feeling decision maker. When I received the letter about my son's accident, I felt my feelings first before I was able to become consciously aware of my thinking about the contents of the letter.

When I had calmed down and was able to think more rationally I realised that I could respond in a number of different ways, and that I could interpret the information in a way that my guidance system told me was negative, or I could choose an interpretation which had a different emotional result. The task for me, in this instance was to get choose the thoughts which resonated and made me feel emotionally sound again.

Does this mean that people who prefer to make decisions from a thinking place are better off? Well sometimes they can be and at other times they can make decisions without being aware of, or ignoring their emotional guidance system in place. The emotional reaction can come at a later stage.

> *Some us feel first, then become of aware of*
> *our thinking and some of us think first, then*
> *become aware of our feelings*

I have seen more conflicts arise in the workplace because some people prefer to live their lives logically, thinking things through and applying facts, and some people use their feelings and how they feel as a barometer for what they like, dislike, how they relate to others and how they make decisions. The thinking and feeling divide, unless understood and appreciated can cause havoc.

Some of you may have come across the book "Men are from Mars – Women are from Venus" by John Gray. The book aims to help male/female relationships by analysing the different ways "Thinkers and Feelers" communicate". It can seem a little stereotypical because it assumes that men are thinkers and women are feelers. And frankly that's not always true, as you know.

Now everyone is able to use both thinking and feeling to inform decisions, we just usually have a preference one way or another.

As we mature, we usually are able to learn our less preferred way, and fingers crossed end up being fairly balanced.

Just to be clear though. Our emotions are based on what we think about something. We take in information, we process it, and then we interpret the information. Depending on whether our interpretation is a negative one, or a positive one, will decide on how we feel about it. Often our processing is so instantaneous and/or unconscious that we don't know why we feel that way. For people with a thinking preference, the thinking comes first. For people with a feeling preference, the feelings come first.

Great emotional intelligence means making decisions from the heart

Many people talk about making decisions from the heart. This can sometimes interpreted as making decisions based on what we feel. However, I believe that decisions from the heart are made when our thinking and feelings are aligned, the alignment resonates with our true self and we feel positive. Or in other words, your thoughts about an event, person or situation are in alignment with your natural state of happiness, peace and forgiveness and your emotions reflect that, and you feel peaceful and happy.

The information that our emotions are a guidance system letting us know whether or not our thinking is in alignment with our true happy state is very useful information. If we regularly experience negative emotions, then we have the key to unlocking the door to happiness. But as the saying goes, "you can lead a horse to water, but you can't make it drink".

Do you want to be right? Or do you want to be happy? It is a choice

There will be a number of people who will not believe that our emotions are a not a valid response or a call to action, and therefore no progress can be made, unless they make the ultimate choice we all have to make at some point, which is: Do you want to be right? Or do you want to be happy? Choosing different ways of thinking to be happy is definitely the road less travelled. Which leads us to the next secret which is that, reacting will lead to the same old results, pausing will let you choose your response.

PEOPLE
DISCOVERY

SECRET 3

Secret 3 - Reacting will lead to the same old results – Pausing will let you choose your response

A friend of mine came off the phone to her daughter. She looked concerned. I asked her what was wrong. She told me that her daughter had handed in her notice at work because she didn't get on with the boss. I could see she was worried. I tried to placate her and said if she was really unhappy and if her boss wasn't going anywhere, then maybe it was the right thing and surely another job would come along soon?

Her concern wasn't though about this incident. It was that this was the third job her daughter had given up in two years, and all for the same reason. She didn't get on with the boss. I had to admit that it was something of a coincidence to have a succession of three bosses who she didn't get on with. Apart from anything else, that would be really unlucky! Seriously though, my friend was worried that it wasn't anything to do with her daughter's boss, but her daughter's reaction to an authority figure.

> *We develop a pattern of reacting, which leads*
> *to the same events happening again*

We all develop habits of reacting to people, situations and events. I know someone who had serious financial problems at a stage in their life. Although they got through this, and thrived afterwards; whenever they received an unexpected bill they still had a negative emotional reaction to this event. The negative emotion was anchored to the receiving of a bill, even though they could comfortably pay any bill, having become quite wealthy.

There is a logical sequence to our reactions. The diagram below shows the process or cycle we follow. The process is sometimes unconscious, and so sometimes we can find ourselves at a stage in the process without consciously knowing why.

How we process information

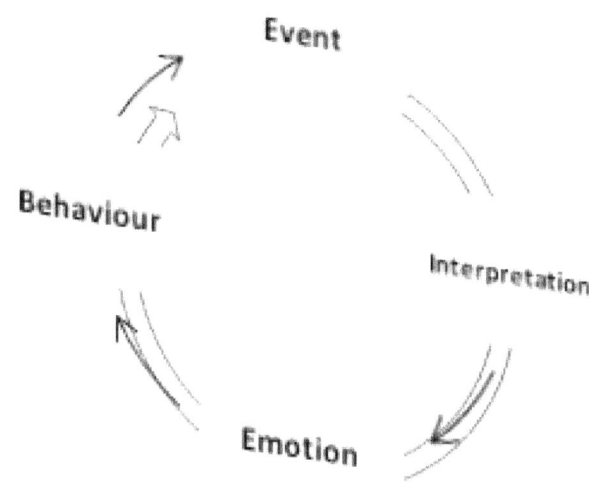

1. Events evoke thought/interpretation
2. Our thoughts determine how we feel (emotions).

3. Emotions in turn affect how we behave.
4. We have thoughts and interpret the emotions we feel and the behaviour we display. This further interpretation can either compound any negative feeling, or increase our happiness if our interpretation is a positive one.
5. How we react will then impact our situation; Behaviours stemming from positive emotions lead to happy, peaceful outcomes. Behaviours which lead from negative emotions can lead to a worsening of the situation or event, and the cycle is perpetuated.

In order to change this cycle, we need to take some time out at the interpretation stage. So the person with financial problems would at the interpretation stage, instead of thinking "Oh no here's a nasty old bill, if this continues, I might be ruined again" May think instead: " Another bill, boy, am I grateful that I have more than enough money to pay this easily, am I lucky? Or am I lucky?" Which would make you feel better? No prizes for guessing.

Below is a diagram of the theory model, with a built in pause at the interpretation stage. Pausing before you react is the first step to brilliant emotional intelligence. Using this secret will demonstrate vividly to you how you are always able to change the way you feel about something by coming up with a better feeling thought.

How we process information

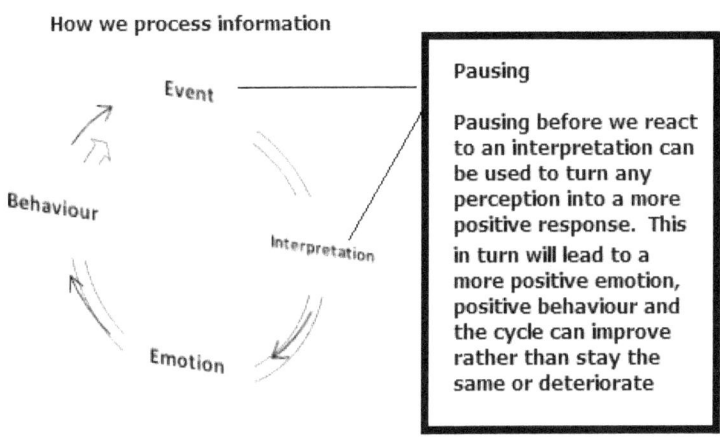

Event

Behaviour

Interpretation

Emotion

Pausing

Pausing before we react to an interpretation can be used to turn any perception into a more positive response. This in turn will lead to a more positive emotion, positive behaviour and the cycle can improve rather than stay the same or deteriorate

Pausing before you react, with the intention of coming up with a better feeling thought is the key to developing your intention to always respond, rather than react, in a positive way. Responding in a positive way is always in alignment with our true selves.

> *Reaching better feeling thoughts and therefore feeling better is a process and you need to climb up the ladder of emotions in stages*

If you are in a state of dark emotions, and have been immersed in negative thinking for a period of time, then it can take some time to get to a state of thinking and therefore feeling better. The process of thinking and therefore feeling better is a gradual

event. The process can take a few seconds, a few days or even a
few months. It much depends on how embedded or fixed your
thinking and beliefs are which have caused the negative emotion.

Below is what I call "The emotional Climb" which is a ladder of
emotions. The ladder can be used to firstly determine where we
are, and secondly as a goal to achieve better feelings, if we are
committed to aligning ourselves with our true selves.

THE EMOTIONAL CLIMB

1									Joy Love Inspiration
2								Passion, Enthusiasm	
3							Peace, Happiness		
4						Appreciation, Gratitude			
5					Purposefulness, motivated				
6				Optimism, Hopefulness, Contentment					
7			Boredom, Pessimism, Impatience						
8			Overwhelmed, Disappointment, Doubt, Irritation						
9		Discouragement, Blame, Worry							
10		Revenge, Anger							
11	Jealousy, Hatred, Rage								
12	Insecurity, Guilt, Unworthiness								
13	Fear, Grief, Depression, Despair, Powerlessness								

Let's work through an illustration of how the ladder can be used.

John had recently taken £1000 out of the bank to pay cash for a
second hand car. The private owner had insisted on cash. On
his way home from the bank, John lost his wallet with the money
in it. Despite doing everything he could, retracing his steps,
calling the police, it seemed the wallet was gone for ever. He

was devastated. Anyone would be. It would be very difficult for John to suddenly feel positive about such an event.

What we have been conditioned to do is think about the event. In this case John was obviously thinking about losing his money. His emotions were fluctuating around steps 9 and 12. He felt down and discouraged, blamed himself and was angry.

If he continued to think about losing his money, without changing his thoughts about the situation, then he might end up in a cycle of negativity, blaming himself, feeling angry and full of recrimination.

He might over time, end up repressing his thoughts and feelings, and just "forgetting" about losing the money, to bring some relief from his negative thoughts and therefore feelings. The trouble with that approach is that every time he remembers losing the money, he could instantly return to his negative state.

If however, he decided that he wanted to actually feel better about losing the money, then the road to healing his emotions about the event would be the focus of his intention.

Thus he might say to himself: "This is an awful blow, but you know, sometimes bad things happen, and people make mistakes". He might then go up a step on the ladder. Then he might say. Actually, it was a truly devastating mistake, but I am really lucky, I have a lovely supportive wife, and two gorgeous kids, I am going to put this event into perspective and realise how lucky I am". Then he goes up another step on the ladder.

If John was feeling the full force of his initial negative thinking, Its unlikely (without a lot of practice) that he would be able to move from the lower rungs up to Step 1 which is joy, love and inspiration quickly. But if he were willing to heal his thinking and feeling about losing the money, instead of burying or repressing his thoughts and feelings about it, then he can truly eventually put the whole event into perspective and not let it worry him any further.

I have to stress at this stage, if you or someone else is thinking and feeling really negative about a situation, you must remember that those feelings are valid! Whatever you are feeling is a response to your thoughts, beliefs and ideas about the situation. By truly embracing your emotions, you can choose to maintain the beliefs, thoughts and feelings which make you feel negative, or you can choose to heal the negative beliefs, thoughts and feelings, which bring you back into alignment with your true self. It is a personal choice. Remember though that all your emotions are a gift, whether negative or not, because they give you valuable information about whether you are aligned with your true self or not.

So in order to practice emotional intelligence we can take ourselves out of the cycle and find a better feeling thought. If you practice this regularly, you will develop your own ladder, stepping up to better feeling thoughts to bring yourself in alignment with your true self. This takes a little practice and self-discipline, but it also leads us to the next secret which is that detachment is the key to great connection.

PEOPLE
DISCOVERY

SECRET 4

Secret 4 – Detachment is the key to great connection

Life can hook us in. If you have ever been to a film and you get unconsciously immersed in the characters and the storyline, and sometimes you might even cry. Then you know you have become for even a short while attached to the story, even feeling like you were living it.

You can sometimes be in the movie theatre and be so involved that when the film is over you have to blink and remember where you are. Sometimes the drama in our own lives takes over and we can get lost in being attached to the story of our lives, or parts of our lives.

As humans we all become attached at some stage in our lives. As children we become attached to our parents and other caregivers. In this scenario, attachment is seen as extremely healthy and necessary for an infant to grow. According to Attachment theory, insecure attachments in childhood can be damaging to children throughout their lives.

> *As children, attachment is healthy, as adults it never is*

As adults we may also have patterns of attachment, both at home and in the workplace. We can become attached in many ways. Attachments come in all shapes and forms. Sometimes we are attached to other people; sometimes we are attached to particular kinds of situations, or substances for example. Obsessive attachments as we know become addictions. When these kinds of attachments become obvious then we will often seek help.

We can become attached to our beliefs even if they make us unhappy

In our personal lives one of the biggest attachments can be our partner, or our beliefs about the way our life should be. I remember coaching an immensely successful and caring man whose marriage had broken up. He was in absolute despair. He was depressed and many months after separation could not get back his motivation, or any zest for life. I suspected that he must miss his wife very much. Surely such depression had come about because he had felt as if he had lost the love of his life? No, he admitted he was no longer in love with his wife. He also felt that they were both in many ways better off without the marriage.

After a little while he admitted that a few years ago, he had fell in love with another woman. He had not pursued this love interest though, because he believed that marriage should last forever. At that time, his belief served him well and preserved a marriage which he realised had a solid base. But when his wife decided she no longer wanted to be in the marriage; a situation he had no control over. His belief became a big problem for him. His belief that marriage should last forever was literally sapping the life out of him. After a simple reframing of his belief he felt much more optimistic and accepting of his situation.

In the workplace, we can often become attached to a particular culture or a belief about the way things should be done. We can become attached to our perceptions of others and also about how relationships should look in the workplace. People who resist change are usually people who are attached to how things should be.

I have worked with organisations where leaders and managers have become attached to their viewpoints about their employees and their capabilities or lack of them. Or they become attached to an attitude or belief about the information they are receiving.

A number of years ago I worked with a manager, who believed that staff surveys were too much of a snapshot, they gave staff the opportunity to have a dig. They even had the view that only the staff that had a grudge filled in the survey, the more valued workers did not have time to fill in the survey: They were too busy doing "proper" work.

This manager was not a new or narrow minded leader as a rule. Indeed he was a specialist and a very credible senior manager. Despite attempts to try to give him a different insight, he preferred to be right and his view prevailed. His survey results never did improve.

> ***Giving up attachments can give us the flexibility we need to live our lives***

In childhood attachment can bring certainty in an uncertain world. As adults, attachments can bring us pain and suffering, when we have to often with great resistance detach. Or we have to admit that we perhaps were thinking or believing amiss. We can exacerbate the very uncertainty we are trying to stave off.

Adult attachment in any form is unhealthy, whether it is a belief a person or a habit. Often we don't even realise we are attached to something or someone, until we have to face physical, emotional, or intellectual change. An attachment is actually a reaction to fear. It's also human nature, so it's nothing to feel bad about!

So what is the answer? We all need to form relationships with people and situations. We need to build a framework of beliefs and ideas so we can function. Below are some of the ways we can better navigate through our lives.

There are alternative responses to pivot attachments into healthier relationships

As we grow into adults we can recognise when we are attached to people and instead reframe this into healthy connections. Connection is a healthy way of relating without the fear base that attachment signifies. We can intimately connect with our very close relationships. As you connect with others you are freer and are more equal.

If we are attached to objects and habits, for example your car or buying new dresses every month, or your home, then giving up the attachments can cause distress or unhappiness.

In those situations attachments will only become painful when, for example, we are perhaps buying new dresses every month and we lose our job. Or our partner gets a new job and we have to move to Australia and this means giving up the family home.

When we are forced to give up attachments we need to reframe our relationship with them. We must explore other options and be open to something different, but there can be great resistance which can be stressful. If we can achieve a different mindset where we appreciated these things, but our happiness wasn't dependant on them: Then we keep our minds open and avoid unnecessary pain.

We need to let go of our need to be right. Attachment to beliefs, attitudes and ideas and emotional responses can limit our life tremendously. Our reality is shaped by our beliefs. What we focus on becomes our world. By keeping an open mind and being prepared to examine our patterns of reaction, beliefs and thinking: being prepared to change them when necessary; we keep fresh and open to what life brings.

And finally we can be purposefully positive. We need to recognise when we are being negative and how this might be limiting ourselves and others, in our lives and our workplaces. Holding onto negative views and conclusions will ultimately prove us right in the end.

If we could recognise when we are attached and with kindness to ourselves relinquish our attachments and replace them with more caring and mindful alternatives, then our lives would be happier and lighter.

PEOPLE
DISCOVERY

SECRET 5

Secret 5 – Emptying is the only way of truly listening and understanding ourselves and others

The art of emptying is one which not many of us are able to do easily. Emptying is the process of putting aside ones beliefs, preconceived ideas, reactive habits and thoughts in order to take in information which can then viewed through fresh eyes or heard through unbiased and attentive hearing. Great coaches have this ability, as do great leaders.

> *Emptying is the process of putting aside beliefs, ideas, habits and thoughts*

We are complex beings. We are bombarded with millions of pieces of information in every moment. We filter out much of this information otherwise we would not be able to cope. The filters that we use to capture information we want are: our beliefs, our ideas, our needs, focus and thoughts as well as our feelings. We are constantly getting information through our 5 senses and our intuition.

We are the sum total of our experiences, our psychological type and our beliefs about the world and our inner desires. We are all therefore unique and different. In other words we all view and interpret information from a different perspective. Quite often we can think we are on the same wavelength with another only to find out somewhere along the line that actually we have come to the same conclusion for different reasons.

Emotionally intelligent people understand that people will think, feel and have different beliefs, and experiences from them, and that is ok. They also respect other peoples' right to have and follow through on their perspective. When they are trying to understand another, they are perfectly content to truly listen, putting aside their filters and preconceived ideas.

I remember a time when I was talking to a colleague about a project we were doing. I explained my stance and she recapped back to me what we were doing and the report she was tasked to produce. I thought that we were on the same wavelength completely. When I received her completed report, I couldn't believe that we were at such odds with each other about our expectations about what the report would look like. I realised that I had made many assumptions about what our common knowledge and experience looked like, and that I had made a big communication gaff. We got together again, and instead of doing most of the talking, I listened intently and we were finally able to both understand what we wanted to achieve.

We are all at different stages of our emotional, intellectual and physical development and accepting this is a true sign of emotional intelligence.

I remember an employee conduct issue I dealt with a number of years ago. On the face of it, the evidence against the employee looked damaging. I deliberately cleared myself of any preconceived ideas I might have formed when I interviewed him. I found out a lot of information which I may not have been open to, had I gone in with my mind already made up. The result was that I decided to shelve the complaint against him, and gained a renewed understanding about him as a person.

I have seen a number of leaders who have formed preconceived ideas about people, and end up reacting to their preconceived ideas, which in some cases bear no resemblance to the actual truth of the matter. People who have difficulty expressing themselves can sometimes come over particularly negatively. An emotionally intelligent person will be able to empty themselves of their judgements about the negativity and drill down to the real problem. It is being open and willing to truly listen.

Emptying means putting aside our values also, something we can find difficult to do. I met a coach who was relating a story about her coaching experience with a young entrepreneur. She had been helping the young business woman make decisions about her commercial ventures. One day the entrepreneur surprised the coach by asking for help to follow her dream and be a model. The coach was concerned that her client was going down the wrong path. She seemed to want to throw away her education, her business experience and the great career opportunities for the future.

It was clear to me that the coach was struggling with her own values, against the best interests of helping her client realise her dream. It sounds obvious but we often make judgements about others based on our values. True emptying means respecting others values while still remaining true to your own. It can be easier said than done!

We can benefit from emptying as a process to help ourselves. When we feel overwhelmed, tired or simply have too much on our minds, I have found three effective ways we can use to clear our minds, thus emptying ourselves to renew our energy. Everyone is different, but for me I use:

Writing - If I have a problem and I'm not sure what to do, or if I have a negative emotional reaction to a situation or someone, I get out my notebook and start writing. It is a great way to clear your mind and get things in perspective.

Breathing – One of the quickest ways to get clear is to simply stop thinking and to breathe. If you concentrate on your breathing then you can't be thinking thoughts which may be overwhelming you or disturbing your peace. Quite often when I am beginning to feel uptight, I realise how tense I am, and often end up breathing shallowly. Relaxing, clearing my mind and focusing on my breathing for 5 minutes or so can be a real relief to the thoughts and information bombarding my mind.

Meditation - is a way of getting in touch with our true selves without the clutter and cacophony of our worries, ideas, conflicting beliefs or even negative emotions. It is a longer process than the quick breathing action, but it entails emptying your mind for up to half an hour. It is best done sitting up and can take some practice.

The art of meditation in particular helps us to get in touch with our intuition, which leads us to the next and final secret of great emotional intelligence, which is that true empathy lets other people be themselves and understands that other people have to listen to their own inner guidance.

50

PEOPLE
DISCOVERY

SECRET 6

Secret 6 – True Empathy understands that other people have to listen to their own guidance

When my daughter was 16, she was unsure about the path she wanted to take. I was really worried about her future. Those of you who are parents will I am sure be with me on this. She decided she was going to leave school. By this time, I was really concerned. We had endless discussions about what she was going to do and the implications for her. Worn down (I later found out), she finally agreed that she would go to college. I was relieved and put the whole situation to the back of my mind.

About 3 months later, I had a call from her tutor at college. My daughter hadn't been attending; in fact she hadn't been seen for about 3 weeks. I calmly told the tutor that she wouldn't be coming back and that I would ask my daughter to confirm this later. I waited for my daughter to come home "from college" I asked her how her day had been and she said fine. I then told her about the call from college, and she burst into tears.

> *We must refrain from projecting our own needs, fears values and desires onto others*

I was really saddened to realise that my own concern about her future had forced her into making a decision which was against her own inner guidance. I decided to completely empty myself of my fears, ideas and concerns. I asked her what she wanted to do. She was very clear she wanted to work in fashion retail. I was gutted. She went for an interview a week later immediately got the job and within 3 months she was made a supervisor at the tender age of 16. She has just recently completed her degree, having gone to university when she decided she wanted to do it.

Great leaders and managers trust their people to use their own inner guidance

One of the most empowering pieces of advice I heard when I was managing was that it was best to let my team take calculated risks.

Sometimes your team might have great ideas about how to achieve something and you might not always agree. An emotionally intelligent leader will trust their team to listen to their own inner guidance and they will be interested to learn their thoughts and feelings about either new initiatives or innovative ways to get things done.

Similarly it is not always a good idea to be the person with all the answers. With my teams I knew that collectively they needed to have an input to the most important decisions. I encouraged my team to be honest and challenging. Sometimes I agreed and as a result of what they told me I would change course, and sometimes I would stick to my guns. Also if one of my team struggled with a problem, I would encourage them to consider and find their own solutions in a very supportive environment. I rarely made decisions without consulting with the people who were involved the most. I know it sounds obvious, but it doesn't always happen.

As a coach, both independently and as a manager with a coaching style, I knew only too well that it is empowering, respectful and honest to let others ask themselves the right questions and to come to an answer that resonated with their own inner guidance.

Life happens and people have problems both at work and at home

People you work with have problems, they have lives and families and relationships and sometimes they have difficult decisions to make. I remember a lady who was on my team who was going through a really messy divorce. She had some time off and I was sympathetic. She had more time off and I became empathetic. I knew that the event she was experiencing was giving her an opportunity to grow. Whether she took it as such or not was entirely a matter for her.

My own objective was to get her back to work because I valued her input. Instead of calling in occupational health or giving her a warning, I talked frankly about the problem I had in that I needed to get the job done, and I wanted her to be the one because it would be difficult to get the quality she contributed from elsewhere. I then asked her to consider what I said and asked if she would be able to come to a solution or find a way to come back to work. She told me to leave it with her, and within 2 weeks she was back to work.

I know that she could have decided otherwise, but I also knew that if that had been the case, then she would have been honouring herself, which as an emotionally intelligent leader, you know is the only decision to be made.

You know yourself that you are the only person who truly knows what is right for you. This is the same for others whether it is your family or your colleagues or team. If you respect that fact and treat people with such respect then you have the basis for a winning and successful family life or team.

And finally, be forgiving of yourself and others on the journey to becoming emotional intelligent.

I hope you have had one or two "aha" moments when you have read the six secrets. There are many other elements to emotional intelligence and lots of information out there. Emotional intelligence is a journey and not a destination and we are all learning. So if you aren't perfect in managing your emotions, then forgive yourself. Also forgive others; they are on the journey the same as you.

If you would like to find out more about great emotional intelligence or simply want to have a chat about how People Discovery might help, then please do contact Christina@peoplediscovery.co.uk; or call 0191 4990070 or 07411765625

PEOPLE
DISCOVERY

www.ingramcontent.com/pod-product-compliance
Lightning Source LLC
Chambersburg PA
CBHW071636170526
45166CB00003B/1338